A Note for You

I0163805

Date: _____

Dear _____

    I am giving you this book because I want to encourage you during this very difficult time. As a Christian, I want to give you some really good news that is found in this book. This will support you in a greater way than anything else I could say or do. I know this gift is a bold step and hope it will not interfere with our relationship. They say the best way to love someone is to tell them the truth, and this book definitely speaks the truth. If you would desire to discuss this book sometime that would be great. If not, that would be fine with me also. Out of respect for your privacy, I will not bring it up.

Sincerely,

_____

PEACE

AMID LIFE'S ANXIOUS MOMENTS

*HOW THE GOSPEL CAN BRING PEACE
TO A WORRIED HEART*

THE FIRST STEP

DONALD E. JONES, PHD

J & A Book Publishers
www.jabookpublishers.com

ISBN-13:978-1946368157
ISBN-10:1946368156

CONTENTS

Chapter 1

Understand and Obtain

One day, when I was a senior pastor, a crying elderly woman entered the church office. Rose explained that she and her husband George had occasionally attended the church years earlier and now he had passed away. Neither of them had been "church people" but she did not know where to go, so she came back to us. She explained that she had been filled with anxiety about many things and leaned on George for support. Though it never fully relieved her, it helped. Without George she had to bear the full weight of her worry alone.

Of course, I agreed to help with the arrangements, the ceremony, and the anxiety. I began to pray privately that as I was assisting her with the funeral arrangements, I could also show her how to find peace for her anxious heart through the gospel of Jesus Christ. Unfortunately, we were both so busy with all that was involved with the funeral that we talked about nothing else.

On the night of the viewing of her husband's body, I sat down next to Rose to comfort her as she greeted her family and friends. At the end of the evening when everyone had gone, there was a moment of silence. She was quietly weeping out of sadness and her hands were quivering out of anxiety and worry. Then a tall, large, muscular man walked into the room and began pacing the room saying in a high-pitched, cracking voice, "I don't know what to say. I don't know what to say." He walked back and forth from the casket to the door, over and over again, still uttering those words, "I don't know what to say." Then, he walked out and never even spoke to us. After this, the silence returned. At that moment, I realized that I did know exactly what to say.

So, I turned to Rose and said, "I leave your dear husband into the hands of a holy, loving God for eternity, but I would like to talk about a solution to your sorrow and anxiety about the future. Would that be okay?" And she grabbed my hand, squeezed it, and agreed as her tears began to flow. And right there in the viewing room, I shared the gospel of Jesus Christ. The same gospel I am about to share with you. When it was over, she had received Jesus Christ as Savior and Lord. I could see a new peace come over her, even in the midst of her sadness, as she placed her life into the hands of God through His Son. After several counseling sessions, her anxiety subsided as her spiritual journey in the Kingdom of God proceeded.

Have you ever wondered why a "good" God who loves mankind would allow such difficulties in our lives? Why would He allow us to feel so much worry inside and in need of such peace? There are many reasons, but an important one is simple and clear: all trials drive us to God. They are meant to shake us up, force us to reason and consider our frailty, and then look upward.

To demonstrate that God would accept anyone who came to Him, Jesus told a tale of a prodigal son. In the story, a son demanded his inheritance from his wealthy father and ran off. He had quite a time living in the luxury and wickedness that money could buy. When he had spent all he had, he became desperate. Then a famine hit the land, and it was so severe that he attached himself to a successful farmer and began tending to his pigs. He was so hungry that he was even willing to eat the pods that the pigs were eating, but no one would allow even this. He was completely alone and in deep trouble. Then one day, he looked upward.

In Luke 15:17-19, Luke records this moment, "But when he came to himself [his senses] he said, 'How many hired servants of my father's have bread enough to spare, and I'm dying with hunger!'" Notice the son can no longer rely upon himself and looks up. Luke continues, "I will get up and go to my father, and will tell him, 'Father, I have sinned against heaven, and in your sight. I am no more worthy to be called your son. Make me as one of your hired servants.'" When the son looked upward, he found his solution in his father. Notice, after all his money had run out, then a famine came. Who brought the famine? The Lord God did. Both of these events put him into the perfect circumstances that would bring him right to his knees before God. This is what He does. At times, He must force us to look up to find Him.

Then Jesus continues by describing the father in the story standing day after day at the edge of town waiting for his son to come home. God is waiting for you to come to Him. When he did arrive in humility and repentance, the Father welcomed him with open arms. In Luke 15:20, Jesus said, "He arose, and came to his father. But while he was still far off, his father saw him, and was moved with compassion, and ran, and fell on his neck, and kissed him." Then, the two went home and celebrated. Through this difficulty, you can be assured that God is calling you to come to Him. Though you may be out of resources, His power is unlimited. He will embrace you, bring you peace, and celebrate your return.

The son would not have looked upward unless his own problems had become so overwhelming that he finally had to ask for divine help from God (represented by his father). This is where you and I must finally be to look up. Lastly, this was a story told by the Lord Jesus who is the only way to heaven. Therefore, when we are compelled to look up to God, we must understand and obtain His Son Jesus Christ by receiving Him as Savior and Lord. This is the good news (the gospel) that will allow you to come home to Him and find the peace you seek.

In John 9:1-12, Jesus encounters a blind man that had been disabled since his birth. Several people asked whether Jesus knew who had sinned to cause his blindness, the man or his parents. In verse 3, John writes, "Jesus answered, 'Neither did this man sin, nor his parents; but, that the works of God might be revealed in him.'" Once his sight was restored, he became a Christian. Two works of God were revealed in this man's life: the healing of his body in sight and his soul in salvation. Had he not been blind, he would not have been healed physically and much more importantly spiritually that day. You can be that wonderful work of God if you will listen, understand, and receive Christ.

I am assuming that this book is in your hands because someone cares about you like I really cared about Rose. This person believes you might be experiencing great anxiety and desires to bring peace into your worried heart. I am also presuming that you have not been able to resolve the anxiety on your own. If this is true, then I have really "good news" for you. Just like Rose, you can fill your worried heart through a relationship with the Lord Jesus Christ that will never end. He will never leave you or forsake you.

Whether you are experiencing this kind of anxiety or not, you still need this book. The gospel of Jesus Christ is the only solution to our eternal problems. Even if we can solve our earthly problems on our own or with help from others, it will not be enough to settle our biggest problem of sin (the breaking of God's law) and our punishment for it (hell for all eternity). You may find some peace here without Him now, but you cannot find any peace without Him after death. In Matthew 16:26, Jesus asked this, "For what will it profit a man, if he gains the whole world, and forfeits his life?" What real profit would it be to find peace on this earth, but forfeit the peace in eternity?

All of us must face the fact that we stand as sinners before a loving but holy God. In Romans 6:23, Paul wrote, "For the wages of sin is death [eternal separation from God], but the free gift of God is eternal life in Christ Jesus our Lord." All have sinned and are condemned (this includes you and me). The good news is that Jesus took care of all our sins on the cross, and we need only to receive Him. This is offered to all, and all may find true salvation through Him alone. We must settle our sin issue first. Then, we will possess eternal peace and will have the power in His Spirit to find it here on earth.

Christ did not die on the cross to primarily meet human needs. In fact, though our needs are important to God, it is not His priority. Why? God is building a kingdom and sent His Son to redeem those who will inhabit it. They must be fit to experience a relationship with Him, serve His Son, and enjoy an eternity of joy and blessing with Him. This can only be accomplished by receiving Christ as our Savior and Lord. The bringing of peace to your worried heart will come as the beautiful consequence, gift, and blessing of knowing, loving, and serving Him.

Will you be open to considering the "good news" of Jesus? Will you attempt to understand Him? If you do and receive Him as Savior and Lord, then you will obtain the peace you so desire, which will fill your heart. Best of all, this good news, which can bring peace, is not based on any man-made philosophies, false religions, secular wisdom, anyone's self-understanding, or even the positive thinking of others but on the truth of God alone found solely in the Scriptures. Will you be open to considering this "good news" of Jesus Christ? Will you keep an open mind as we discuss these many life-changing biblical principles?

This does not imply that Jesus is not concerned about our needs at all. Though we may need suffering to drive us to God, Jesus feels real compassion for the difficulties we face. He not only came to lift our spiritual burdens but to lift our physical, emotional, and psychological ones also. He wants to lift the burden of our anxious hearts, but this will be done in the way that seems right to our God, not us. This is an important distinction. In Matthew 11:28-30, Jesus declared, "Come to me, all you who labor and are heavily burdened, and I will give you rest. Take my yoke upon you, and learn from me, for I am gentle and humble in heart; and you will find rest for your souls. For my yoke is easy, and my burden is light."

This does not mean that all our problems will go away, but we will be able to bear our difficulties more easily with His guidance and power. This will make them feel lighter, and we will find rest in our lives whether trouble comes or not. I do not know what exactly caused your worry, but I know you will find peace in His "rest." To find this rest from your anxiety and worry, you must hear the gospel of Christ and respond to it by becoming a Christian.

This book is entitled "the first step," but you must also take others as well. The next spiritual step will be to grow in your Christian life. This life in the Spirit will aid in the relief of your anxiety. Do not handle this part of your journey alone but seek some help from pastors, counselors, Christian friends, and others. The third step will come from a study of the Bible. These will be dealt with in subsequent books.

Our salvation must come first, so you will have the power through the Holy Spirit to find this peacefulness as you seek help. Those who do not know Christ must rely on their own personal strength. In Ephesians 3:16, Paul prays for his Christian readers to experience this kind of power in their lives, "That he would grant you, according to the riches of his glory, that you may be strengthened with power through his Spirit in the inward man." You can have this real power through Jesus Christ as you pray and read His Word.

The thoughts and feelings you are experiencing might be multifaceted and may require a multifaceted approach. This could include medical, psychological, social, and legal help from those who are experts in their field. This book in no way implies that merely receiving Jesus and even growing in Him is the only solution to the issues you face. I encourage you to begin your spiritual journey with Him and get the additional help you need. Both can be done together. This is what the Bible teaches.

In 2 Chronicles 16, King Asa of Judah had a serious foot disease, and rather than seek God first, he depended solely on the physicians. This angered God, not because he utilized the services of physicians, but because God was left out. In verse 12, the author states, "In the thirty-ninth year of his reign Asa was diseased in his feet; his disease was exceeding great: yet in his disease he didn't seek Yahweh, but to the physicians." The Lord desires to be sought first while one also seeks help from professionals, not them or necessarily Him alone. Seeking Him through His Son is the first step of the spiritual solution. Utilizing professional help may be a prior, simultaneous, or future step.

You might think that you have heard this gospel message before and wonder why you should hear it again. This is because often people hear bits and pieces of the good news but not a complete version based solely from the Scriptures. This takes some time and explanation as you have in this book. I have taken the time to explain it all to you and hope you will read and heed. It is an incredible story that must be told over and over.

One Last Thought:

As a Christian Pastoral Counselor addressing a very serious life problem in this book, I must recognize the possibility that someone might be reading this and contemplating suicide. If this is the case, please do not hesitate to call 911 or go to the nearest emergency room or hospital immediately.

(And take this book with you!)

Chapter 2

Seek and Turn

Since you have decided to hear the gospel of Jesus Christ, we will begin at the very beginning of the world. This will provide a proper perspective on how we should view our struggles in the light of who we are, and why we are here. The first two actions we must take to deal with our difficulty are to seek and turn.

Seek Christ's Kingdom

The first response we should make to bring peace to our worried hearts is to understand the truths concerning the kingdom of God, accept its reality, and then seek it. The gospel of Jesus begins with God's plan of redemption, which was ordained in eternity past and fully revealed to mankind over thousands of years in the Holy Scriptures. It is truly an amazing story of the how and why of our existence. For you to become a Christian and remove the anxiety and worry, you must understand where it came from. It is derived from man's fall, and the solution is found in our redemption in Jesus Christ.

In Genesis chapter two, God described His creation of the earth, sun, moon, stars, plants, and animals. After this, the Lord God proceeded to fashion His greatest creation: man. Here's where we come in. In verse 7, Moses writes that God formed man out of the dust of the ground and then breathed into him the breath of life. As a result, man became a living, thinking being. Out of man, the Lord God formed a woman (Genesis 2:18-25). God placed both the man and woman in a

9

beautiful earthly garden called Eden and walked and talked with the couple in the cool of the day (Genesis 3:8). Though some may think this is a fairy tale, it is not. This true story unlocks the key to why God spent time with them in a deep and abiding relationship.

Why was Adam and Eve created in the first place (which would eventually lead to us)? Why were they walking and talking with God in the garden in the cool of the day? What was the point? These are the same kinds of questions that people have been struggling with for thousands of years. Why do we exist? What is life all about? Am I going to just happen into the world and happen out of the world, and that is it? These answers are found in the Bible. The creation of man was the creation of a kingdom of people by God the Father to honor God the Son. That is right. Our purpose, which will bring peace, is to serve and honor God's Son.

Let me explain. In John 3:35, John the Baptist describes it this way, "The Father loves the Son, and has given [as a gift] all things into his hand." In John 10:29, the Son, Jesus, portrays His people as sheep and states, "My Father, who has given them [as a gift] to me, is greater than all." Then, in Colossians 1:15-16, Paul, the apostle, described it in these words, "Who [Jesus] is the image of the invisible God, the firstborn [preeminent one, not first to be born] of all creation. For by him all things were created, in the heavens and on the earth, things visible and things invisible, whether thrones or dominions or principalities or powers; all things have been created through him, and for him." Notice, the two words stated "for Him." Everything in the universe was created "for Him." This includes us.

So, as Adam and Eve walked in the garden, they were to be given as a love gift to God the Son from God the Father. In Genesis 1:28, this is the reason they were given a powerful mandate by God when the Lord commanded, "Be fruitful, multiply, fill the earth, and subdue it. Have dominion over the fish of the sea, over the birds of the sky, and over every living thing that moves on the earth." The two were to have children with their children having children and so forth until the earth was filled with human beings. The plan was for all mankind to be in control of the planet and develop into one glorious kingdom of God with many people groups who served and honored the Son.

Who would rule man as man ruled the earth? It was to be the Son of God. Why? It was His kingdom, which was a gift from the Father. Then the Son with His kingdom would live their lives glorifying the Father. All would be done in and through the Holy Spirit. This is a mystery and can't be fully understood. This was to be the Triune God (three persons in one essence) at work as they loved each other and us. All would be done forever as men and women continually ate of the tree of Life found in center of the garden (Genesis 2:9). There would be no anxiety or worry here.

In John 17:1-2, as Jesus prays to His Father God before His betrayal, He reveals this gift and plan in His own words, "Jesus said these things, and lifting up his eyes to heaven, he said, 'Father, the time has come. Glorify your Son, that your Son may also glorify you; even as you gave him authority over all flesh, he will give eternal life to all whom you have given him.'" The Father desires to glorify His Son and the Son seeks to glorify His Father.

We often hear people describe God as all-powerful God who is always striving after His own honor and glory, but it is so much deeper than this. God is not a power-hungry ruler who is absolutely desperate for His subjects to honor Him alone; instead, He is a loving God who desires to honor and glorify His Son. God's Son is a loving God who desires

His Father also to be honored. The Holy Spirit is the third divine personhood who desires to see the Father and Son glorified. In John 17, we discover that the Father desired to glorify the Son and He wanted the Son to experience what He had as the Son glorified Him. So, the Father decided to create a kingdom of people who would glorify His Son as the Son glorified Him. He wanted His Son to experience the same relationship He had with the Son with a multitude of His "brothers and sisters."

Therefore, what is our purpose on earth? It is primarily to live as an important part of a kingdom that glorifies (Psalm 86:9), worships (John 4:23), and serves (Luke 4:8) the Son. We (the Son and His brethren) glorify the Father. This is all done in and through the Spirit, which brings all beyond the temporal and mortal to the eternal and immortal. Beyond these purposes people in this kingdom were to fellowship and enjoy interaction with Him, (1 John 1:3; Genesis 3:8) each other, and nature (Genesis 1:29-31). They were to be holy, righteous, and blameless before God (Ephesians 1:4), to understand and experience all of God's attributes (Romans 9:22), to reign and rule over earth in order to honor Him (Genesis 1:28), and to exist forever and ever as His people (Genesis 3:22). This is the essence of resolving the problem of our anxiety: living for God's Son. Our purpose comes not in serving and pleasing ourselves but in serving and pleasing Him.

As can be seen, all this was to occur on our present earth. This kingdom of people would live in a world free of sin, disease, and disharmony. There would never be any anxiety or worry. Mankind would live in perfectly created human bodies, which feasted continuously on the fruit of the Tree of Life for eternity. As mentioned, this fellowship began in a lush garden with just Adam and Eve. Their responsibility was twofold. One, they were to subdue the earth and control it for God's glory. Second, they were to reproduce and then populate the earth filling it with kingdom people who loved the Son.

To aid mankind in his endeavor, God created myriads of angelic beings to not only honor Him but to serve man, as He accomplished this. This would have been our original future here. If Adam and Eve had followed God, we would be on a perfect earth as perfect people loving God and each other perfectly. There would be no problems. We would be happy and calm every moment of eternity. Unfortunately, it did not work out that way.

At first, things went well for the couple as they walked and talked with God in the Garden of Eden. Then, a disaster occurred. As they went forth to subdue the earth, they were given one stipulation. They could enjoy all that they had, as long as they did not eat of one tree in the garden. This tree was known as the Tree of Good and Evil (Genesis 2:16-17). God told them that in the day they disobeyed Him and ate the fruit, they would "die."

In the garden of God was placed a beautiful and powerful angelic being to assist them. Almost immediately, this angel saw all that God was doing for His Son and desired this for himself. Since Lucifer truly wanted the glory, power, and kingdom that were being bestowed on the Son, he rebelled against God and took a third of the angels with him. Then, this fallen one set about to take control over all mankind as soon as he could.

The angel turned himself into the form of a serpent and tempted and deceived Eve, and she ate of the fruit of the Tree of Good and Evil. Adam rebelled and ate the fruit also (Genesis 3:1-7). As a result, all mankind fell and lost all their blessings (1 Corinthians 15:22) including peace.

God had developed a simple yet powerful blueprint for His kingdom people on earth, but now it was over. They would rebel against Him and live their own way. Mankind had fallen into sin, and they would become a part of Satan's (Lucifer) kingdom and follow the Devil (Colossians 1:13). Sin entered the world, and people would now follow after their own lusts, interests, desires, and needs (1 John 2:15-17). The earth was cursed bringing disease, pestilence, and famine into the world (Romans 8:19). People would now physically die and experience all of the problems that accompany it. In the midst of this chaos, man would have to live with the consequences of his own sins and the wickedness of others upon him. This would lead to all of the problems mankind has experienced including what you are now facing.

Of course, the final problem will be our own deaths and final judgment. Mankind would die in their sins bringing an eternity of punishment under the justice and wrath of God (Romans 1:18; Ephesians 2:3; Hebrews 9:27). People would not only experience physical death but spiritual death and punishment for all their sins in a hell of fire (Matthew 5:22). Though our problems are overwhelming at the moment, they will seem like nothing compared to the harsh treatment of eternal punishment.

God could not leave His kingdom in ruin or mankind in this horrific condition, so the plan of redemption came into effect. Before the very foundation of the world, this plan was worked out in eternity past in the mind of the Triune God (Ephesians 1:3-6, 11-12).

This plan took into account man's sin. Though man did not have to, nor should he have, nor did God want him to, yet God knew man would sin. When mankind rebelled, He determined that His divine response would be to pour out upon man more of His love, goodness, mercy, and grace.

14

This would bring greater glory to Him, His Son, and Spirit and an abundance of more blessings for man (Ephesians 1:6).

The Godhead determined that the Second Person of the Trinity would clothe Himself in humanity and come to earth to pay the penalty for man's sin to satisfy God's holiness, justice, and wrath that had been violated (Philippians 2:5-8; Isaiah 53:6). In Romans 3:23-24, the apostle Paul writes, "For all have sinned, and fall short of the glory of God." Every person sins and deserves punishment. Then, Paul continues with the Lord God's solution, "Being justified freely by his grace through the redemption that is in Christ Jesus."

Then the Savior came, was born in a manger, and grew up as the God-man Jesus. For approximately three years, Jesus declared that He was the Son of God and only Savior of the world. He offered Israel and all others the opportunity to become a member of God's kingdom by believing in Him. He performed many miracles and fulfilled many prophecies mentioned in the Old Testament concerning His birth, life, and even death. Jesus Himself also predicted His suffering, death, and resurrection from the dead.

The leaders and people hated the Lord for His teachings, righteousness, and declaration that He was God's Son. They had developed a perfect little man-made works system to get themselves into heaven and refused to believe in the son of a carpenter no matter what He said and did.

Then Jesus was arrested, tried before the Jewish officials, and a Roman leader named Pilate. He handed the innocent God-Man over to be crucified. They nailed Him to the cross, and when the proper time came, He yielded up His spirit and declared, "It is finished" (John 19:31). Three days later, He rose from the dead and was seen by witnesses including over 500 people at one time (1 Corinthians 15:3-11).

Jesus was on earth for forty more days. During this time, He provided many convincing proofs of His resurrection and gave His disciples a divine mission: go and proclaim the gospel, make followers of Him, and teach them all that He taught them. If men believed in Jesus as the one and only Savior of the world and submitted their lives to Him as Lord, they could enter the kingdom of God forever. If men did not receive Him, then they would have to pay their own penalty for their sins by spending an eternity in punishment without God, His Father. Everyone must come individually to Him.

This is the gospel of Jesus Christ. This is the good news of the kingdom of God. Now that you have heard, your first response is to believe in and then seek this kingdom. You must desire to become a member of the kingdom of His Son. When the Lord explained to the people that in His kingdom they did not have to be concerned about clothing and food, Jesus asserted that they should be seeking the kingdom of God instead. This is critical.

In Matthew 6:33, Jesus Christ said, "But seek first God's Kingdom, and his righteousness; and all these things will be given to you as well." In Matthew 13:44, Jesus compared believers who sought His kingdom to a man who found a treasure in a field and with joy sold all he had to obtain it. The Greek word that is translated "seek" means "to crave, demand, and strive after."

As we seek His kingdom, our worry will lessen because we will know that we are seeking an eternity, which is free of anxiety. When the problems of this world are seen in the light of the joy, peace, and blessing we will have forever and ever, our hearts cannot help but feel a sense of great relief as we prepare for the warm, soothing waters of supernatural life through God's Spirit to flow in.

Turn from Sin

Once we decide to seek His kingdom, the next response is to recognize our sin and repent of it. Our sin affects both our lives now and in eternity. Though we have trouble now, we have much more trouble coming. The gospel of Jesus was not intended to solve problems in this life as much as it was intended to solve a terrible problem we have as we face a much longer life in eternity. When we die life does not end, it really begins. Our difficulties now cannot compare to the difficulties we will have if we do not deal with our spiritual problem, which is sin, because our sin leads to an eternity of punishment and sorrow.

Though we may not be cognizant of it every moment, we intuitively know that judgment is coming. The apostle Paul described this sense of our eminent demise as coming from three sources in our lives. First, creation shouts out to us that there is a God and, this God is righteous. It cries out that we are sinners deserving judgment, but we suppress this truth in order to live our own way without Him (Romans 1:18-20). Second, our consciences inside us are constantly judging our every action according to a law God has put within us. This law is constantly condemning our actions, but we ignore it (Romans 2:15). Third, the Holy Spirit is constantly convicting us of our sinfulness and attesting to salvation only in Jesus, but we push Him aside (John 16:8).

In Romans 3:10-11, Paul explains that there is no one who is righteous or understands God. In Romans 3:23, he asserts that all have sinned and fall short of God's glory. This sin brought God's condemnation. Then in chapter 6:23, Paul writes, "For the wages of sin is death." This death refers to both physical and eternal death separation from God. Since this truth is preached by the Lord Jesus and His apostles in every gospel message, I must preach it to you.

Though people think Jesus preached only love, this is not the case. He indicted people for their wickedness. When Jesus was seated at a well and waiting, for the disciples to purchase food for their journey, He encountered a woman who came to draw water. He told her that He had living water (the gospel), which she could drink, that would spring up to eternal life. When she requested this living water, He began to confront her wicked living. In John 4:16-18, Christ responded with a scathing description of her sin, "Jesus said to her, 'Go, call your husband, and come here.' The woman answered, 'I have no husband.' Jesus said to her, 'You said well, 'I have no husband,' for you have had five husbands; and he whom you now have is not your husband. This you have said truly.'" He did not yell or berate her; He gently confronted her in order to give her the perfect opportunity to repent of her many sins. The indictment of sin was never to crush people but to offer salvation through repentance.

In John 8, evil men came and cast an adulterous woman in front of Jesus and asked Him if she should be stoned to death. Jesus responded by writing their sins on the ground with a stick and asked those who were sinless to cast the first stone. These accusers needed to deal with their own sins before they dealt with hers. They refused and left leaving the woman there alone.

In John 8:11, the Lord commanded the adulterous woman to "Go your way. From now on, sin no more." The Lord did not attempt to conceal the woman's sin or theirs. This entire scene involved the exposure of the sins of people and the opportunity to find salvation through the Lord Jesus, not condemnation. Eternal judgment comes when people refuse to recognize their sin and embrace Jesus as Saviour and Lord so their sins can be forgiven. We must know that there will be no second chance. In Hebrews 9:27, the author says that people die once then judgment comes.

So, what is this judgment of sin to come? Though hinted at in the Old Testament, Jesus Christ clearly explained a future punishment to come in a place called "Hell.". The Lord Jesus did speak of God's love, grace, and mercy, but Christ also declared that all must repent of their wickedness and believe in Him (Matthew 4:17; Mark 1:15). If not, they would go to a place of "unquenchable fire" (Matthew 3:12; Mark 9:43; Luke 3:17). It was a supernatural dwelling with an eternal inferno (Matthew 18:8) where weeping (from the sorrow and pain endured constantly) and gnashing of teeth (from agony and anguish of suffering and torment forever) exist continually without relief (Matthew 8:12; 13:42, 50; 22:13; 24:51; 25:30; Luke 13:28).

Why must man face this punishment? The key is found in Revelation 4:10. Here, John discloses that those in hell "will drink of the wine of the wrath of God." This wine will be "prepared unmixed in the cup of His anger." The Almighty God of the universe is angry, and mankind must be saved through Him or experience His wrath for all eternity. Why is God so angry? People hear all the time about the love, grace, and mercy of God but rarely His holiness, righteousness, and justice.

These key attributes are just as much a part of His divine nature as His love, grace, and mercy. This has made people think that our God is only wonderful and sweet and never wrathful, but this is not so! As mankind views himself as a composite of many attributes, God must be seen in the same way. God is angry because He Himself and His laws are righteous, holy, and just, but human constantly refuse to honor God, His Son, or follow His laws (Psalm 89:14,18). As a result, these attributes of God absolutely demand a penalty to be paid for their sin (Romans 1:18; 2:5). There can be no way around this; no matter how much love God may have for man, the love itself cannot satisfy the demand.

19

Due to mankind's horrible condition, His love, grace, and mercy surfaced, and a divine provision was made. Someone else would take mankind's place and bear his penalty for sin. Someone who never transgressed Him, who never deserved punishment, and fulfilled the entire law of God, would be substituted in rebellious man's place to receive this awful punishment from God. This person would be born, live, and experience God's full wrath to satisfy His justice for sin (John 1:29; 3:16; Hebrews 9:22). This substitute would have to be divine for it to be eternal and supernatural. He would have to be human for it to be a true replacement. So, the Son took on human flesh to die for us (John 1:1, 14).

As the God-Man, He paid the penalty for our sins in His death on the cross. God made only one provision for people to appropriate what His Son did on the cross for them. This provision is the repentance of sin and faith in Jesus Christ as only Savior of the world and Lord of their lives. People must stand humbly before this holy, righteous, and just God and acknowledge that God is full of anger and wrath for their constant, continual sin and disobedience. They must repent of their wickedness and receive Jesus Christ as Savior and Lord. They must believe He is God's Son and only Savior of the world. They must ask Him to save them and submit their lives to Him as Lord and Master.

This repentance involves simply admitting that we have sinned (1 John 1:8,10), sorrowing over it (2 Corinthians 7:9-10), and turning toward righteous living (Luke 22:62). It isn't so much confessing every deed, even if we knew them all, but acknowledging we are sinners and committing ourselves in God's power to turn from all sins as God convicts us now and in the future. This repentance before our God will have a powerful effect on our troubled hearts as we finally deal with the sin, judgment, and the dread that are contributing to it. Most of all, it leads to an eternity of blessing with God.

Chapter 3

Believe and Receive

Once we have decided to seek His kingdom and repent of our sins, we are ready for the next two actions, which must be taken in our journey toward temporal and eternal peace. These two responses, which will deal with our anxiety now and provide an eternal future with God, are to believe and receive.

Believe in Christ's Deity

To have a relationship with God through His only Son, we must believe that Jesus Christ is the Son of God. We must believe in His deity. What does this mean? There are three persons in one Godhead or three personalities in one deity (Matthew 3:16-17; Ephesians 2:18; 1 Peter 1:2). We call this the Trinity (Tri-unity): Father, Son, and Holy Spirit. Though the word "Trinity" is not in the Bible, this truth is explained clearly. Therefore, the true gospel message concerns itself with the proclamation that Jesus is God's Son. This means He is deity who is equal with the Father.

In John 8:58, Christ told the Jews that before Abraham was born, He existed (I Am). This is Christ's direct claim to be the God or Yahweh (I Am) of the Old Testament. The Jewish people knew this and took up stones to kill Him for blasphemy. Jesus claimed to be God; this was blasphemy of the highest order to them. Had Jesus proclaimed to be only a good prophet or great teacher as some thought He was, they would have reacted differently (John 8:59). Some say Jesus was a prophet or teacher, but He claimed to be God.

21

In Mark 14:61, Jesus stood before the Sanhedrin. When asked if He was the Christ, the Son of the Blessed One, He replied with the "I Am." This was the designation of Yahweh of the Old Testament. The high priest's response was the tearing of his robes to signify blasphemy. Declaring oneself to be the Son of God was a pronouncement of deity. In John 10:30, when Jesus declared that He and the Father were one (essence), He was proclaiming His deity.

The apostles also proclaimed the deity of Jesus. In Acts 2:36, Peter proclaimed, "Let all the house of Israel therefore know certainly that God [the Father] has made him both Lord and Christ, this Jesus whom you crucified." Here, he was speaking before a huge crowd at Pentecost and declared that Jesus was both Lord and Christ. In Acts 3:14-15, Peter healed the lame man and proclaimed that Jesus was the Holy and Righteous One and the Prince of Life. These many designations refer to His deity first and foremost. In Acts 4:12, Peter boldly announced to the Sanhedrin that only in the name of Jesus could one be saved! This can only be done by deity. In Acts 8, the eunuch from Ethiopia was reading a messianic passage from Isaiah. Philip, an evangelist in the early church, revealed that it referred to the risen Jesus as the Messiah. This was a proclamation of His deity.

To be saved, our response must be belief in Christ's deity. No one can be saved unless that person believes Jesus Christ is God, one with the Father as His Only Son (John 8:58-59; 10:30). The passage, which verifies this important truth, is in John 3:16. Here Jesus declared, "For God so loved the world [mankind], that he gave his one and only Son, that whoever believes in him should not perish, but have eternal life." Someone must "believe." John finishes his proclamation of the gospel in his book by declaring that Jesus had performed many other signs. These were not written in the gospel, but the ones written were to prove that Jesus is the Christ, the

Son of God (John 20:30-31). God did not expect anyone to simply believe blindly but gave powerful evidence, which His Holy Spirit utilizes to convince and confirm this in our hearts. We will see these later. Therefore, eternal life comes from believing that Christ is the Son. To find the peace you desire, you must believe Jesus is the Son of God.

Receive Christ as Savior

Jesus Christ is God's Son and the only Savior of the world. To make the next response, we must believe that Jesus died on the cross for our sins and receive Him as only Savior of the world. In Luke 19:10, Jesus Himself said that He had come to save all those who were lost. In Matthew 1:21, an angel of the Lord told Joseph to name the baby that was in Mary's womb "Jesus" because He would save His people from their sins. In Romans 5:8-11, the apostle Paul wrote that Christians were saved by His death on the cross, justified by His blood, reconciled to God, and delivered from the wrath to come. Though deliverance from our anxiety now through God's peace might be a wonderful result, it should not be our primary concern. Our main issue is delivering us from the anxiety and fear of a terrifying eternity.

In 1 John 4:14, the apostle, proclaimed, "We have seen and testify that the Father has sent the Son as the Savior of the world." Jesus saves people from their sins through His death on the cross. In Colossians 2:13, Paul explained, "You were dead through your trespasses and the uncircumcision of your flesh. He made you alive together with him, having forgiven us all our trespasses." Because of what Jesus Christ did on the cross, we are saved through His total forgiveness of all our sins. This means that all our sins from the past, in the present, and those we have not yet committed in the future are forgiven fully and completely.

23

This belief implies that He is God's only provision for sin. In John 14:6, John records the words Jesus said clearly to Peter, "Jesus said to him, 'I am the way, the truth, and the life. No one comes to the Father, except through me." In Acts 4:12, Peter had fully understood His declaration because he proclaimed to the Jewish leaders, "There is salvation in none other, for neither is there any other name under heaven, that is given among men, by which we must be saved!" We are accused of being too narrow, but this came directly from Christ. I am merely repeating what Jesus directly said, which was heard and confirmed by His apostles.

For you to attain His forgiveness and find the peace you desire, you must receive Jesus Christ as only Savior of the world. What does "receive" mean? In John 1:12, John refers to our relationship with Jesus Christ in these words, "But as many as received him, to them he gave the right to become God's children, to those who believe in his name." The Greek word translated "receive" means "to take." In the context of a person, it refers "to taking with the hand, laying hold of any person or thing in order to use it, or to make it one's own." It has the idea of giving someone access to oneself in a person-to-person relationship. It is a relationship word. To receive Christ, we take His hand and bring Him into our lives as He takes our hand and does the same.

In John 6:21, this term was used immediately after the disciples saw Jesus walking on the water and received Him into the boat. As they received Him into the boat, you are to receive Him into your life. In John 19:27, while on the cross, Jesus asked John to care for His mother. From that day on, she was received into his household, and Mary became a part of his family. In the same way, when Christ is received by people, they enter into a familial relationship with Him. This believing and receiving Jesus Christ brings forgiveness and forgiveness can bring peace now and forever.

Chapter 4

Submit and Affirm

As we continue in our understanding of the gospel, it is important to note that these truths found in the Bible may take time to fully understand and then believe. Please take all that you need; it is a life-changing decision. There are two additional actions which we must take in order to become Christians and align ourselves with God's blueprint. These are to submit and affirm.

Submit to Christ as Lord

The next key response we must take to bring peace to our anxious hearts is to submit to Jesus as Lord. This speaks of Christ's authority in relation to believers. People are to enter into a covenant of obedience to Jesus. We must understand that Jesus Christ is not only our Savior but also the Lord. It is important to note that the key word referring to Jesus in the New Testament is the "Lord," literally meaning "Master."

In Matthew 3:3, the author, describes John the Baptist as preparing the way for "the Lord." In Matthew 7:20, Jesus refers to Himself as "Lord." This title implies obedience. In Matthew 28:18, before Jesus Christ ascended into heaven, He declared, "All authority has been given to me in heaven and on earth." This refers to Christ's Lordship over everything. In Colossians 1:16, Paul states the following, "For by him all things were created, in the heavens and on the earth, things visible and things invisible, whether thrones or dominions or principalities or powers [angelic beings]; all things have been created through him and for him." This is about Him!

There are numerous passages in the New Testament in which the Lord Jesus not only declared but demonstrated His full authority over nature (John 6:16-21; Mark 11:12-20), sin (Mark 2:5; Luke 7:49), disease (Matthew 4:23-24; Luke 6:17-19), angels (Hebrews 1:4,6,13), demons (Matthew 8:16), unbelievers (1 Timothy 6:15); His church (Colossians 1:18; Romans 8:29), and even physical death (John 11:17-44; Luke 7:14). The Lordship of Jesus is a critical part of you finding the peace you are searching for and must not be left out. In Acts 2:36, Peter declared that all of Israel needed to know God had made Jesus both the Christ and Lord. Both terms for Jesus are used. In Acts 4:33, Luke describes the disciples proclaiming the good news as testimony to the resurrection of the "Lord." They declared Jesus to be the Lord.

In Acts 11:20, witnessing is termed "preaching the Lord Jesus." Luke writes, "But there were some of them, men of Cyprus and Cyrene, who, when they had come to Antioch, spoke to the Hellenists, preaching the Lord Jesus." In Acts 13:12, the gospel is also called the preaching of the Lord. In Ephesians 1:20-23, Paul asserts that Christ is the Lord of all. He is the only one with the authority to save, judge, and rule forever. Jesus Christ is the only one with the right to demand allegiance and command obedience. This is a crucial element of the gospel because it produces the obedience that is the foundation of the true Christian life and the secret to peace.

Making Jesus Lord of your life changes your perspective and orientation. To become a Christian, you must turn your whole life over to a new master. You must relinquish the control of your own life and submit to Him as Master as you grow in your obedience to Christ. In Matthew 10:39, Jesus declared, "He who seeks his life will lose it; and he who loses his life for my sake will find it." This means we must give up our self-directed life for a life directed by the Lord Jesus in His Word. We are to no longer live to please ourselves but

Him, and peace ensues. This is not a complete and absolute obedience but the desire and pursuit of it. This begins at salvation with submission to His Lordship. To begin to rid ourselves of our anxiety, we turn our lives over to Him.

Affirm Christ's Resurrection

As was mentioned earlier, the Holy Spirit has chosen to provide evidence of Christ's deity which He will use to bring us to belief in Jesus Christ as the Son of God. Finding real peace in our lives cannot be based on some inspirational experience or feelings but on a person, who is Jesus Christ confirmed by powerful evidence created by God Himself. Here are some, which should be met with an affirmation of Christ's resurrection to be saved.

To prove His divinity Jesus did many miracles, fulfilled many prophecies (both Old Testament and His own), and rose from the dead. Of course, His resurrection from death itself was his greatest miracle and fulfillment of prophecy. How could anything be greater than rising from the dead? The Lord God spent thousands of years creating these signs and evidence and wants it to be declared to you.

First, as Jesus preached the kingdom, He performed many miracles to confirm His deity and message. In Matthew 4:23, the apostle records that the Lord proclaimed the gospel and then healed the sick. This was His usual method of sharing the gospel. The Lord would proclaim His deity and prove it through miracles. In Matthew 11:4-6, when John the Baptist sent his followers to inquire about Christ's deity, Jesus spoke of the miracles that He performed: He healed the sick, made the lame walk, and caused the blind to see, the deaf to hear, and the mute to speak. In John 5:36, the Lord challenged the Jewish people to consider the works (miracles) He had done as a testimony to His deity. He never appealed to some inner experience they should have had with Him.

Second, Jesus fulfilled numerous prophecies in order to demonstrate that He was the Son of God. In this way, the world would be able to identify God's Son in human flesh. These signs and prophecies were provided by God primarily through the prophets of Israel. Over many years, these men would speak of God's judgment on Israel for their sins, and then His future blessing through the sending of His Son and their Messiah (Anointed One). The Lord Jesus fulfilled these prophecies in several ways. Most, He fulfilled them through God's providence (Micah 5:2; Psalm 72:10; Jeremiah 31:15; Hosea 11:1; Isaiah 9:1-2). This means God determined where He was to be born, etc. Others, Christ fulfilled intentionally and deliberately (Luke 4:21; John 2:22; 13:18; 17:12; 19:28). Then Jesus Himself also predicted events that would occur during the final week of His earthly life (Matthew 26:1-2, 6-12; John 3:14-15; 8:28-29; 12:23-24).

Third, the Lord resurrected from the dead and fulfilled numerous prophecies demonstrating exactly who He was. It is critical to note that His resurrection was predicted in the Old Testament (Job 19:25-26; Psalm 16:8-11; 22:19-24; Isaiah 53:10-11) and it was fulfilled with much evidence in the New Testament (1 Corinthians 15:5-11; Matthew 28:9-10). Luke begins his book of Acts by stating that the Lord Jesus Christ appeared to His disciples after His resurrection for a period of forty days and provided many proofs to them that He was truly alive from the dead (Acts 1:3).

Since rising from the dead is such a powerful testimony, let us consider for a moment the circumstances surrounding His death, burial, and resurrection, and how God confirmed this important truth. Since only the Romans could judge and condemn a man to death, the Jews brought Him before the

Roman governor whose name was Pilate. Though he tried to dissuade them, they would not stop calling for his death. So, the Lord condemned and crucified on a cross (the most humiliating, excruciating, and agonizing death). Once dead, two of His secret disciples asked permission to take the body and bury it properly. They placed His body into one of their own empty tombs. Since the Jews feared the disciples would probably steal His physical body and claim Jesus resurrected from the dead, they begged the governor to seal the tomb and post guards in front of it (probably sixteen).

The massive stone covering the tomb would have been approximately two tons and rolled into place by a gulley they dug. In spite of all the precautions and security, by the third day the body was gone, and Jesus had risen just as He Himself had predicted. Immediately, Jesus began to appear to His disciples and others for many days to make sure the world knew that He had risen from the dead. Paul tells us He had even appeared to over five hundred people at one time (1 Corinthians 15:6).

Not only did Jesus proclaim His deity and demonstrate it through His miracles, His fulfillment of prophecy, and His resurrection, but His disciples were told to proclaim what they had seen of Him. They were commanded to share His message and the proofs of His deity to those in Jerusalem, Judea, Samaria, and all the earth (Acts 1:8). This is exactly what they did. He told them they would be His "witnesses." They were simply to share what they had seen and heard. The book of Acts was written to show how this was done not only by the apostles but all Christians.

Since Christians today are not eyewitnesses, how do we confirm and defend our faith to you? Consider Luke, who also was not an eyewitness of Jesus Christ. In Luke 1:1-4, the author explains that he investigated all that had happened from actual eye-witness accounts. This way all who read His gospel would know with certainty that Christ was the Son of God. Now, as a disciple of Jesus Christ, I am reading their eye-witness testimony and presenting it to you!

Your response to the defense of the deity of Jesus should be the firm belief that Christ is the Son of God (deity) from the miracles, fulfilled prophecies, and His resurrection from the dead. Since I did not quote each of the passages I cited, I encourage you to obtain a Bible and read it for yourself. The biblical response to this is an affirmation of the resurrection. In Romans 10:9, Paul explains, "That if you will confess with your mouth that Jesus is Lord, and believe in your heart that God raised him from the dead, you will be saved." In 1 Corinthians 15, Paul gives the essence of the gospel: Christ died, was buried, and rose again according to the Scriptures (verses 3-4).

This belief will come through the power of the Holy Spirit working in your heart as I have presented the evidence to you, and you have studied them for yourself. So, to discover peace through salvation in Jesus Christ, you must submit to Him and affirm His resurrection.

Chapter 5

Love and Depend

The next two responses to finding salvation are to love Christ and depend upon Him. Herein lies real peace for our worried hearts. Why? When we have a relationship with the living Christ that is characterized by real love, we can have victory over any problem, difficulty, or issue. In 1 John 4:10, John states, "In this is love, not that we loved God, but that he loved us, and sent his Son as the atoning sacrifice for our sins." In this, we will discover a powerful sense of peace.

Love Christ in a Relationship

Christ isn't simply an historical man of the past, nor is He a distant God of the present but the God-Man, risen, alive, and desirous of a real relationship with people. The essence of Christianity is not just obeying a list of precepts but, more importantly, interacting with a divine person. Though the Scriptures don't utilize the word relationship, they assume it. They describe our relationship with the Triune God using a variety of analogies to speak of the many facets of this love.

The Scriptures speak of Christians as children of a holy Father (Romans 8:15; 2 Thessalonians 2:16-17), as brides of a loving groom (Ephesians 5:25-32), as siblings of a devoted brother (Mark 10:28-29), as friends of a sacrificial companion (John 15:13-14); as servants of a benevolent master (Romans 1:1; Revelation 19:5), as subjects of a great king (Revelation 19:15-16), as sheep of a righteous shepherd (John 10:1-10), as branches on a healthy vine (John 15:5-6) and as a spiritual body with a divine head (Colossians 1:18).

31

In Revelation, Jesus discussed His relationship with two churches. In Revelation 2:4, the Lord accused the church at Ephesus of departing from their first love. Their motivation in their persistence and endurance was no longer love for Him. True Christians are in love with Jesus Christ. This is an authentic relationship. What does this word "love" really mean? The Greek word that is translated "love" is defined as "valuing or prizing someone or something." It is not seen as a romantic word but a word that speaks of commitment and devotion. We are committed and devoted children, wives, siblings, friends, branches, subjects, and sheep.

The main characteristic of this devotion and commitment is obedience to His Word. In John 14:15, Jesus defines it, "If you love me, keep my commandments." In verse 21, the Lord adds, "One who has my commandments, and keeps them, that person is one who loves me. One who loves me will be loved by my Father, and I will love him, and will reveal myself to him." In verse 24, Jesus compares this to the person who does not love Him, "He who doesn't love me doesn't keep my words." Just so we know that this teaching comes directly from the Father, Jesus continues, "The word which you hear isn't mine, but the Father's who sent me." This would include the entire Bible (John 17:17; 2 Peter 3:16).

In Revelation 3:16, Jesus charges the church in Laodicea with being lukewarm (neither hot nor cold) toward Him. In verse 20, the Lord offers those in the church a relationship with Him when he proclaims that He is standing at the door and knocking. If people in the church "hear" His voice and "open" the door, He will "dine" with them. Each one of these terms signifies relationships.

In 1 John 1:3, John indicates that he proclaimed the gospel to them so they could fellowship with the Lord Jesus Christ. He describes it in this way, "That which we have seen and heard we declare to you, that you also may have fellowship with us. Yes and our fellowship is with the Father, and with his Son, Jesus Christ." The word "fellowship" speaks of a relationship. It means participation in a partnership. This is what you must do to be saved. You enter into a partnership with Christ and participate in the plan of your Lord and Master. This does not refer to working your way into God's grace in order to enter His heaven. It simply refers to the fact that Christians realize and acknowledge that they are in a love relationship with a living God, not a dead prophet, and this pours forth into obedience.

Our love for Christ must reign supreme above all other earthly pursuits (pleasure, occupation, sports, etc.). It must be first above the love we have for ourselves and all others. Once again, herein lies one of the keys to finding faith and mercy. Christians love their Lord and live first for Him. He isn't an add-on to living how we desire. This isn't God's way.

The kingdom of God was created for His Son not man's joy and pleasure. We live to please our Lord first. We can enjoy the many things that this world offers as long as it does not include disobedience to Christ's commandments. None can dominate our pursuits or relationships above Him. We must count this cost! To find salvation, you must make a commitment to love Jesus. To love Jesus Christ in the kind of relationship God desires is the path to peace.

Depend on Faith Alone

Salvation is by faith alone, not by any good works. People cannot work their way into God's heaven. Good works are always a result of salvation. Over and over, the Lord Jesus Christ declared that one must believe in Him as God (His Son) to be saved. In John 4:39, John describes the salvation of a group of people, who had been brought to the well by the Samaritan woman, as believing in Him. In John 6:29, Jesus told His listeners that they must believe in Him whom God sent. In John 6:35, Jesus declared that He was the bread of life, and they must believe in Him for eternal life. There are many Bible passages that teach this important truth.

The apostles proclaimed the same powerful truth. In Acts 4:4, Luke describes those who were saved as those who had believed. In Acts 8:37, when the eunuch from Ethiopia heard the gospel, he confessed that he believed Jesus Christ was the Son of God. Peter, the apostle, preached to Cornelius that anyone who believes in Christ receives forgiveness of sins. In Acts 16:36, Paul told the Philippian jailer and all in his household that they must believe in the Lord Jesus Christ to be saved. Belief in Jesus alone was constantly proclaimed. Over and over Jesus declared belief without works to save.

The Lord Jesus spoke often concerning the producing of fruit in keeping with true faith. Good works are the result of faith. In Matthew 13:23, the Lord Jesus compared believers to seeds that always produce the fruit of righteous deeds by their faith. In John 15:2, Jesus compares Himself to a vine, and His true followers are those branches that produce real fruit. If His branches abide in Him, they will bear much fruit, because apart from Him they can do nothing (John 15:5). As a result, faith which cannot be seen by obedience to God in right living is a dead faith and cannot save (James 2:14-17).

So, to be saved, we must believe that faith alone will save us. In Ephesians 2:8-10, Paul clearly explains that salvation is a result of faith, not works. Why? So, no man is able to boast before God. No one will ever be able to claim that he worked his way into heaven. He continues by explaining that we are God's workmanship created for good works. Faith leading to good works will bring peace.

Chapter 6

Accept and Proclaim

Once we receive Jesus Christ as Savior and Lord, there are two more responses God desires His new children to make. These are to accept and proclaim. These two actions will add much to finding the peace we seek.

Accept God's Forgiveness

The next action is obvious but must be mentioned. Once the Lord God forgives all our sins, we must actually accept His forgiveness and forgive ourselves. Sometimes, we are held back because we think we are too sinful or wicked to forgive. This simply is not true. What Jesus Christ did on the cross was powerful enough to forgive any sin and all sins. We merely have to accept God's forgiveness by faith with a sense of blessing and gratefulness. This can bring a deep sense of peace. Here is an awe-inspiring truth: the moment we repent and receive Jesus as our Savior and Lord then all of our past, present, and future sins and the punishment that accompanies them are washed away.

What does this mean? At the moment that we place our faith in Jesus, the penalties for all our sins, which were paid at the cross, are now appropriated to us directly. Eternal life became ours with full, complete, and total forgiveness of sin. We claim this by faith. This will produce peace!

In John 19:30, the apostle heard and recorded the Lord's final words just before His death, "When Jesus therefore had received the vinegar, he said, 'It is finished.' Jesus bowed his head, and gave up his spirit." The three words translated "it is finished" is actually one word in the Greek meaning "to finish, complete." This important word was used in secular life as a contractual term meaning "payment in full."

In ancient times, someone would borrow money and sign a contract. When any debt was paid off, it was stamped "Payment in Full." We often see this same phrase stamped on receipts today. The debt for our sins was fully paid on the cross. As His life was pouring out, Jesus was declaring, "The penalty is now paid in full." Jesus had come to suffer and die for us, to pay all the debts of our sin and punishment, and it was completed. As soon as Jesus Christ uttered these words, He gave up His spirit (John 19:30). When we receive Christ, our penalty is paid. Your debts are gone. We are free! Will not peace ensue?

Paul deepens our concept of what happened on the cross in Colossians 2. In verses 13-14, Paul explained, "You were dead in your trespasses and the uncircumcision of your flesh. He made you alive together with him, having forgiven us all our trespasses, wiping out the certificate of debt which was decrees against us; and he has taken it out of the way, nailing it to the cross" (DEJ). Christ has taken the certificate of debt consisting of decrees against us, and He has nailed them to the cross. What are these "decrees?" The decrees are the many judgments against us for every transgression we ever committed, are committing, or will ever commit. Our sins are written in books that Christ will open on the day of final judgment with most likely the precise name, date, and time of every single sin we ever committed.

In Ephesians 1:7-8, Paul explains what Jesus was able to accomplish, "In whom we have our redemption through his blood, the forgiveness of all our trespasses, according to the riches of his grace, which he made to abound toward us in all wisdom and prudence." So, once we receive Jesus Christ, we merely claim by faith His full forgiveness of all our sins. When this momentous event occurs, will not peace flood our worried hearts?

Proclaim Christ in Baptism

The second of these two responses is to proclaim to all our newfound faith in Christ through water baptism. In the New Testament, full immersion into water (baptism) was continually declared and practiced as the first response after one receives Jesus as Savior and Lord. People would believe, and then they would be baptized. This was also the pattern of Jesus Christ and the apostles in their proclamation of the good news. In John 3:22, John, the apostle, records that the Lord Jesus was in the land of Judea baptizing. Obviously, this occurred after the preaching of the kingdom, which is always described by the gospel writers as Christ's message of redemption (Matthew 4:17; Mark 1:15; Luke 8:1). Again, people would believe, and then they were baptized. Jesus was preaching the kingdom, and His disciples baptized all who received Him (John 4:2). In Matthew 28:18-20, the risen Jesus commanded His disciples "to make disciples" by going, then baptizing, and finally teaching others.

In Acts 2:41, after the people received Peter's word (the gospel) and believed in Christ, they were baptized. Though this would have been a momentous undertaking, more than three thousand people were saved and baptized that day. In Acts 8:12-13, Luke records that once some of the citizens of Samaria were saved, Philip baptized them. Then in Acts 8:35-36, Philip is sent to the Ethiopian eunuch and shared the good news with him. As soon as this high official believed, he asked Philip to be baptized. How did the eunuch know this? Philip must have explained this truth of water baptism during his presentation of the gospel. The truth of baptism was definitely a part of his message.

In Acts 10:47, once Cornelius, the centurion, and all of his household had professed Christ as their Savior and Lord, Peter ordered them to be baptized, and they were. In Acts 16:15, Lydia and her household believed and were baptized. A few verses later in Acts 16:33, the jailer and his household believed and were also baptized. In Acts 22:16, after Paul became a Christian, he was commanded by Christ soon after to be baptized.

Then what is baptism, and how is it linked to salvation? This is our first response of obedience to Jesus as Lord, not for salvation itself. This water baptism does not and cannot save us, but it will announce our belief in who Jesus is, and what He did on the cross for us. This honors and glorifies the Son the way His Father God so desires. Water baptism is a powerful outward symbol of the supernatural reality of our new birth in Christ.

The immersion in the water was to signify that they had died to their old lives and been raised to new ones through Jesus Christ's death and resurrection (Romans 6:4). The Lord Jesus Christ desires for His people to announce their newly obtained salvation to the saints and the world through this outward sign. Only believers' were being baptized and never babies based on the faith of their parents. Think of how beautiful it is to share with the world not only our salvation but newfound sense of peace.

Chapter 7

Enjoy and Anticipate

Once we are saved, we have only to enjoy the blessings of our salvation and to anticipate our final rewards. This will add greatly to the peace that we desire. In John 10:10, Jesus spoke of Himself as the true shepherd in contrast to thieves (false prophets and teachers) who come to pillage the sheep. He declared, "The thief only comes to steal, kill, and destroy. I came that they may have life, and may have it abundantly." This offer deals primarily with our spiritual lives now and heavenly lives in eternity that will free us from anxiety.

Enjoy God's Blessings

God has given all believers spiritual blessings from now and into eternity. First, our standing before Almighty God has changed. Paul states that through Christ believers in Him are justified before the Lord (Romans 5:1). This means that we are given the righteousness of Jesus Christ and then declared righteous before God (Romans 4:6). There is no condemnation for any sin we have ever committed or will commit (Romans 8:1, 33-34; 5:16). We are fully at peace with the God of the universe (John 14:27).

Second, our identity has changed. We entered a living and abiding relationship with God as our Father (Romans 8:15). We become the brothers and sisters of Jesus (Matthew 12:49), and each other (1 Peter 3:8) and are a part of a new family of God (John 1:12). In 1 Peter 2:9, Peter describes us in this way, "But you are a chosen race, a royal priesthood, a holy nation, a people for God's own possession." We finally have found a place to belong! We are part of the family of God serving Him as chosen, royal, holy priests, possessions, and a nation. Who on earth has a better purpose than this?

Third, our being has changed. In 2 Corinthians 5:17, Paul says, "Therefore if anyone is in Christ, he is a new creation. The old things have passed away. Behold, all things have become new." The word "new" means "brand new, new of a different kind." Our old inner person and ways of thinking, feeling, and doing becomes brand new. We have a new inner person. We begin a life-long transformation into becoming Christ-like. We are spiritually alive and able to understand the things of God (Ephesians 2:1; 2 Corinthians 2:14).

Fourth, our bondage to sin has changed. What do I mean by this? Unbelievers are living in the domain or kingdom of darkness (Colossians 1:12-13). This domain is ruled by the prince of the power of the air who is the Devil (Ephesians 2:2). They are slaves of sin and wickedness following after the lusts of the flesh (Romans 6:6; 1 Peter 4:3). Their father is Satan himself (John 8:44) being His children (1 John 3:10). After receiving Jesus as Savior and Lord, we are transferred from the domain of darkness into the kingdom of Christ. We are now able to overcome sin and live righteously (Romans 6:14-22; 8:13). Of course, this will not be perfect as long as we have these old bodies that continually entice us (Romans 7:5, 24), but we are freed from sin's death grip.

Fifth, our attitude toward all our trials and problems has changed. We are not shielded from many of life's difficulties, but we know that no matter what happens everything will work toward our good and the good of others through God's power (Romans 8:28). Trauma will come to demonstrate our faith in Christ and to push and prod us toward maturity in Him (James 1:2). During these moments, we can rely upon God's strength to endure with joy and dignity (Philippians

4:13; 2 Corinthians 12:8-10). Most of all, we no longer fear death, because it is now the doorway to the greatest blessing, which is heaven itself (Hebrews 2:15; Philippians 1:19). In the midst of it all, we will always be able to go to the throne of God boldly to petition Him, for whatever we may need during these difficult times (1 John 3:21-22; James 1:5).

Sixth, our relationships to others have changed. We have become an important part of the church, the Body of Christ (1 Corinthians 12:27). The believers in the church of Jesus Christ are meant to mutually support one another as each one attempts to live for Him on this earth. We become your new spiritual family (Matthew 12:49; John 1:12). As a result, we together are to love one another (John 13:34), accept one another (Romans 15:17), serve one another (Galatians 5:13), carry each other's many burdens (Galatians 6:2), forgive one another (Colossians 3:16), be kind to one another (Ephesians 4:32), warn one another to keep from harm (Romans 15:14), and encourage one another (Hebrews 10:24). These are just a few of the ways in which God's family takes care of its own.

Seventh, our direction in life has changed. We are now caught up in the greatest purpose for which people can live, and that is building up the kingdom of God on earth as we await the coming of Jesus Christ (James 5:7-8; Revelation 3:11). This "building" has several aspects. The first one is the physical advancement of Jesus Christ's kingdom through sharing the gospel (Acts 1:8). The second is the spiritual growth of the church by sharing in ministry and service (1 Corinthians 12-14). The third is to raise up families who are dedicated to the Lord Jesus (Ephesians 6:4). If single, these saints have the privilege of being singularly devoted to the Lord (1 Corinthians 7:32). The fourth is personally growing in the knowledge and wisdom of the Lord (1 Peter 2:2; 1 John 2:13-14). The knowledge and experience of these kinds of blessings can produce in us the peace we desire.

Eighth, we find joy. Right now, you may experience the pleasure of sins such as partying, drunkenness, and other behaviors (1 John 2:16). You are participating in the delights of the earth such as sunsets and beaches (Psalm 4:7). You are also involved in the "fun" of human activities such as sports and hobbies. You hopefully have found happiness in various relationships such as with friends, spouses, and children. The sinful pleasures won't satisfy. The other two will come and go, but Christians experience the joy of God that lasts. It is a divine joy, and one that we can pursue. In Philippians 4:4, Paul says, "Rejoice in the Lord always! Again, I will say, 'Rejoice!'" Here Paul commands Christians to find their joy in the Lord Jesus. We can have constant joy if we pursue Him and know Jesus is available at all times. Will not the knowledge and experience of these blessings produce in us the peace we desire?

Anticipate Our Inheritance

Another response that produces peace is to anticipate a future inheritance. When we receive Jesus, our eternity will change. We will become possessors of eternal life. We won't have to worry about the Lord God judging the "goods" and "bads" of our lives on a divine scale and then casting us into everlasting joy or fire. This is a myth. One is either a saint (holy one separated to God) or one is not (separated from God). In 1 John 5:11-12, John wrote, "He who has [possesses] the Son has [possesses] the life. He who doesn't have God's Son doesn't have the life. These things I have written to you who believe in the name of the Son of God, that you may know that you have eternal life, and that you may continue to believe in the name of the Son of God." Those who have the Son have eternal life. This inheritance is given on the day of salvation. Our recognition of this possession as we look forward to heaven should bring much peace.

42

We have discussed our earthy blessings that are a part of this eternal life; now, we move on to our eternal blessings after death. This is referred to as heaven: the dwelling place of God. This is our inheritance as Christians (Ephesians 1:11) and we are to anticipate and look forward to it (James 5:7). This blessing has two aspects to it. The first is the privilege of living with our God and His Son in His Spirit forever and ever. The second is the honor of being rewarded for the many good and righteous works that we have done on earth. This would refer to any good done for the sake of Christ.

The Holy Scriptures give us only a glimpse of heaven. In a few places the curtain of mystery is pulled back, and we are provided a most dazzling display of this heavenly abode where the throne of God Almighty dwells (Isaiah 6:1; Ezekiel 1:26; Daniel 7:9). This heaven (dwelling place of God) will someday intersect with a new heavens (universe) and earth. In the center will be the throne of the Lord God dwelling in a New Jerusalem (Revelation 21:1-4).

The next aspect is the reward that we will receive for our obedience to the Lord. In 2 Corinthians 5:10, Paul describes this, "For we must all be revealed before the judgment seat of Christ; that each one may receive the things in the body, according to what he has done, whether good or bad [not sinful but useless]." There will be no punishment for our sins because they are forgiven. There will be no rewards for the many neutral actions and activities we may be involved in on earth (hobbies, activities, sports), but we will only receive rewards for the good deeds we have done for Christ.

These rewards are explained in numerous places in the Scriptures. First, we will have clothing bearing our deeds. In Revelation 19:7-8, John describes it in these words, "'Let us rejoice and be exceedingly glad, and let us give the glory to him. For the marriage of the Lamb has come, and his wife has made herself ready.' It was given to her that she would array herself in bright, pure, fine linen: for the fine linen is the righteous acts of the saints." We, as saints, will enjoy a great feast with the Lord Jesus Christ wearing white robes decorated with our righteous deeds listed on them.

The Scriptures describe various crowns we will be given. The word used refers not to the crowns kings wore, but the wreaths of honor victors in athletic games wore. There are five major wreaths of honor mentioned: the incorruptible crown (1 Corinthians 9:25-27), the crown of rejoicing (Daniel 12:3; 1 Thess. 2:19-20), the crown of life (Revelation 2:10; James 1:2-3), the crown of righteousness (2 Timothy 4:8), and the crown of glory (Acts 20:26-28, 1 Pet. 5:2-4). These are a taste of the heavenly blessings given to us.

In the book of Revelation, John describes a series of very personal rewards that believers will receive. A few of these rewards are described by Christ Himself. They will consist of being given a white stone with a new name written on it (Revelation 2:17), the confessing of our names as His before God the Father and His angels (Revelation 3:5), becoming spiritual pillars in the heavenly temple with the name of our God, the city of God, and Christ's new name emblazoned upon us (Revelation 3:12), and sitting at the very throne of Christ (Revelation 3:21). In Revelation 21:7, Jesus concludes, "He who overcomes, I will give him these things. I will be his God, and he will be my son."

In summary, our sinful, wicked deeds are forgiven and, our good deeds from faith are rewarded. There will be no rewards for the numerous neutral actions and activities we became involved in on this earth (hobbies, activities, sports). These are just a small taste of the heavenly blessings we have in store for us. This anticipation of our future reward can rid ourselves of our anxiety and bring peace.

Chapter 8

Live and Serve

Though the issues you are facing may be very complex, much of the solution might be found in living the "Christian life" the way God truly desires for us to live. Following His blueprint once we are saved can help us approach many of the problems of life in a more powerful way. It provides a new set of tools (spiritual truths) for dealing with them. These principles from the Scriptures actually constitute the second step in this recovery and healing process, which will be dealt with in a forthcoming book. A third book (the third step) will follow, which includes specific biblical principles that address your difficulty if the first two steps do not fully solve them. Some may or may not need a second or third step because everyone is different.

Live Our New Life for Christ

Once we receive Christ, we begin a journey of honoring and glorifying Christ from the moment of salvation on earth and into eternity in heaven. This involves growing into mature saints as we await heaven. In Ephesians 4:13, Paul describes the goal of the church on earth as attaining to the unity of the faith and of the knowledge of the Son of God. Christians do this both individually and corporately until we become full grown and mature in Christ. This means we are to measure up to the "stature of the fullness of Christ." This would be like a brother standing next to his older brother attempting to grow into his image. We are standing next to Jesus and growing into His image constantly checking our character, attitudes, and lifestyle.

How does this actually occur? The answer is so simple. If Jesus Christ was dependent on our God, then we learn to be dependent on God also. If Christ was patient, we learn to be patient. If Christ obeyed God's commands, we learn to obey God's commands. For our study in this chapter, this spiritual growth process into the image of Christ consists of scriptural study, intercessory prayer, fellowship with the saints, sound instruction, ministering one's gifts, sharing the gospel, living righteously, and enduring trials. As I mentioned previously a fuller explanation with additional principles will follow the publication of this book.

Let's take each of these briefly. If you become a believer, God desires that you read His Bible regularly. Why? This is how He speaks to His people. So, believers need a consistent time of study in the Bible. It is the Word of God that the Holy Spirit uses to transform you into Christ's image. In 1 Thessalonians 2:13, the apostle Paul explains how the Bible works in lives, "For this cause we also thank God without ceasing, that, when you received from us the word of the message of God, you accepted it not as the word of men, but, as it is in truth, the word of God, which also works in you who believe."

In a relationship, not only are we to allow God to talk to us, but we are to talk to Him. This is called prayer. In 1 John 5:14, the apostle John describes prayer as boldly being in the presence of God face to face and communicating with Him. In many of Paul's letters, he asks for prayer (Colossians 4:3-5) and requests that the saints pray for others (Ephesians 6:18). In fact, in 1 Thessalonians 5:17, the apostle encourages Christians to never stop praying. Praying is a critical part of the Christian life and assists us in our spiritual growth as we depend upon God to meet our needs. In study and prayer, we find solutions to problems and the strength to handle them. This provides peace!

Serve Others for the Lord

The next response will encompass service to others in a variety of ways. It is not "me" centered but Christ centered, which compels us to serve others in the church and outside the church. Here are a few aspects of this. Christians are to fellowship with other believers. The apostle John uses this word to describe the interaction of the saints. In 1 John 1:6-7, he speaks of our "fellowship" with one another. The Greek word connotes a "joint participation." We are involved in a joint participation in the advancement of the Kingdom of God and the spiritual maturing of the saints. The primary way we do this is to love, serve, encourage, warn, teach, and build up one another (John 13:34; Romans 14:15; Galatians 5:13; 1 Thessalonians 4:18; 5:11; Colossians 3:16).

Christians need to be taught the truths in the Scriptures. This is called teaching "sound doctrine." God has placed within the church pastor-teachers who instruct the saints in sound doctrine to equip them to serve the saints in the church (Ephesians 4:11-12). Personal study of the Scriptures is profitable, but a strong teacher of the Word can provide the deeper truths and their applications to our lives.

Another aspect of the Christian life is what I am doing with you now, which is sharing the gospel. In Acts 1:8, Jesus left the disciples with these words, "But you will receive power when the Holy Spirit has come upon you. You will be witnesses to me in Jerusalem, in all Judea and Samaria, and to the uttermost parts of the earth." God has given to the church evangelists to train Christians to share their faith.

Another aspect of being in the kingdom of God is living righteously. In Colossians 1:10, Paul describes our Christian lives, "So that you will walk in a manner worthy of the Lord, to please Him [Christ] in all respects, bearing fruit in every good work and increasing in the knowledge of God." We are to walk about in our daily lives moment by moment in a manner that is worthy of the Lord. How do we do this? We commit ourselves to demonstrating our love for Jesus Christ by living righteously.

All of these spiritual pursuits should bring much of the peace you are searching for. I cannot claim that it will deal with everything you are experiencing. With these aspects of living and serving, the Lord only expects whatever you are realistically able to do. In order to deal with this truly heavy burden emotionally, you might still need some professional help; this is perfectly fine and can be necessary at times. Often Timothy relied on Paul for help in His life while he was experiencing many difficulties. I encourage you to take this first step, try these aspects of living and serving and at the same time please, seek the needed help.

Conclusion

We come to the end of my presentation of the gospel of Jesus Christ. You now have all that you need to receive Him and experience the peace of salvation and relief of anxiety or reject Him and continue in condemnation. I only ask that you take time to fully consider these truths. If and when you might desire to receive Him, you can pray this prayer:

Dear God,

> *I want to be a part of your Son's kingdom. I know that all I deserve is judgment for my sin. I am so sorry for what I have done. I believe Jesus is your Son. I know this because he resurrected from the dead. I believe that He died on the cross to pay the penalty for my sin. I believe that He is the only way to heaven. I welcome and receive Him into my life right now as Savior. I turn my life over to Him as Lord. I want a love relationship with Jesus Christ. I thank you for the blessings you are bestowing on me right now. I am so grateful for this peace in my life, which was gained by the faith your Spirit gave me and not by any works. I will do my best to live for you and fulfill the purpose for which I have been created.*

If you prayed that prayer of commitment then the Holy Spirit has entered you, and you are now a child of God. You should begin feeling more peaceful and less worried as you claim the Lord's forgiveness by faith. That peace may come either quickly or slowly, but it will indeed come. You should immediately find a bible teaching church and begin your adventure in the Kingdom of God and your journey to full relief. There will be times you will worry, but they should lessen as you grow in your relationship with the Lord.

I would suggest you get a copy of the Bible and begin reading the gospel of John. As you read, just enjoy your time with the Lord as if you were walking with Him along those dusty roads. If this is too difficult to understand at first, then get a copy of a paraphrase Bible which is not literal but will give you a beginner's sense of the kingdom you are a part of.

If you choose to take some time to really understand these truths, then read through the book again and look up the passages. You may also simply read the gospel of John. It is all there. If you decide to reject Jesus Christ, please realize that giving you this book was a deeply caring act from the one who gave it to you. Remember, as the father waited for the return of his prodigal son, so God will wait for us while we live.

Please understand and be warned that once death comes, then comes judgment. In Hebrews 9:27, the author warns all of us, "In as much as it is appointed for men to die once, and after this, judgment." This means we will not have a second chance after death. I leave you with the most well-known verse in the world. It is John 3:16, "For God so loved the world, that he gave his one and only Son, that whoever believes in him should not perish, but have eternal life." I hope I will see you in heaven!

A Final Thought:

If you are suicidal, please call 911 or go to an emergency room or hospital immediately.

(And take this book with you!)

ABOUT THE AUTHOR

Dr. Donald Jones is currently a Christian Pastoral Counselor with thirty-eight years of experience in the fields of pastoral ministry, public education, and Christian counseling. He carries degrees and certificates from four major universities and from a variety of educational institutions. He has been a professor of Languages and Bible, a television commentator, and a featured speaker at a variety of events and seminars at churches, schools, and other organizations across the United States. He is a member in good standing of several secular and Christian professional organizations. Dr. Jones has been a published author since 1976. For further information view his website at www.donjonesphd.com.